THE BIG BOOK OF
POLITICS
QUOTES

Curated by M.K.

"Politicians and diapers must be changed often, and for the same reason."

— Mark Twain

"It's not the people who vote that count. It's the people who count the votes."

— Joseph Stalin

"If you do not take an interest in the affairs of your government, then you are doomed to live under the rule of fools."

— Plato

"A nation which can prefer disgrace to danger is prepared for a master, and deserves one."

— Alexander Hamilton

"He who would trade liberty for some temporary security, deserves neither liberty nor security."

— Benjamin Franklin

"Poverty is the parent of revolution and crime."

— Aristotle

"Nothing is easier than to denounce the evildoer; nothing is more difficult than to understand him."

— Fyodor Dostoevsky

"Every record has been destroyed or falsified, every book has been rewritten, every picture has been repainted, every statue and street building has been renamed, every date has been altered. And that process is continuing day be day and minute by minute. History has stopped. Nothing exists except the endless present in which the party is always right."

— George Orwell

"In politics, nothing happens by accident. If it happens, you can bet it was planned that way."

— Franklin D. Roosevelt

"Power will be maintained by the groovy guy or gal who gets the most media coverage for his sleaze. Naturally, his friends in various businesses will do okay, too."

— Frank Zappa

"Fascism is capitalism in decay."

— Vladimir Lenin

"Somebody has to do something, and it's just incredibly pathetic that it has to be us."

— Jerry Garcia

"Always stand on principle even if you stand alone."

— John Adams

"If socialists understood economics,
they wouldn't be socialist."

— Friedrich August von Hayek

"There is no word more "dangerous" than liberalism, because to oppose it is the new "unforgivable sin. "."

— Fulton J. Sheen

"I've told you before and I'll tell you again. The strong survive and the weak disappear. We do not intend to disappear."

— Jimmy Hoffa

"What is the difference between a cactus and a conservative caucus? On a cactus, the pricks are on the outside."

— John Diefenbaker

"When you can't make them see the light, make them feel the heat."

— Ronald Reagan

"Republican is fine, if your a millionaire. Democrats is fair, if all you own is what you wear. Neither of them's really right, cause neither of them care."

— Frank Zappa

"The American Constitution was not written to protect criminals; it was written to protect the government from becoming criminals."

— Lenny Bruce

"The press must grow day in and day out - it is our Party's sharpest and most powerful weapon."

— Joseph Stalin

"Enlightened statesmen will not always be at the helm."

— James Madison

"The more we do to you, the less you seem to believe we are doing it."

— Josef Mengele

"The world is now too small for anything but brotherhood."

— A. Powell Davies

"The Tories, every election, must have a bogy man. If you haven't got a programme, a bogy man will do."

— Aneurin Bevan

"We have a theoretical concept of the Revolution which is a dictatorship of the exploited against the exploiters."

— Fidel Castro

"The main vice of capitalism is the uneven distribution of prosperity. The main vice of socialism is the even distribution of misery."

— Winston Churchill

"When dictatorship is a fact, revolution becomes a right."

— Victor Hugo

"The oppressed are allowed once every few years to decide which particular representatives of the oppressing class are to represent and repress them in parliament."

— Vladimir Lenin

"Liberals, it has been said, are generous with other peoples' money, except when it comes to questions of national survival when they prefer to be generous with other people's freedom and security."

— William F. Buckley, Jr.

"Mankind will never see an end of trouble until lovers of wisdom come to hold political power, or the holders of power become lovers of wisdom."

— Plato

"The socialized state is to justice, order, and freedom what the Marquis de Sade is to love."

— William F. Buckley, Jr.

"Never make a defense or apology before you are accused."

— Charles I of England

"The world is governed by opinion."

— Thomas Hobbes

"Democrats are the only reason to vote for Republicans."

— Will Rogers

"A government is an institution that holds a monopoly on the legitimate use of violence."

— Max Weber

"When it becomes serious, you have to lie."

— Jean-Claude Juncker

"Communism has defeated itself everywhere except. in American colleges."

— Paul Harvey

"A Conservative is a fellow who is standing athwart history yelling 'Stop!'."

— William F. Buckley, Jr.

"To change masters is not to be free."

— Jose Marti

"Politics and hypocrites is turning us all into lunatics."

— Marvin Gaye

"I have come to the conclusion that politics are too serious a matter to be left to the politicians."

— Charles de Gaulle

"Fascism is definitely and absolutely opposed to the doctrines of liberalism, both in the political and economic sphere."

— Benito Mussolini

"Skip the religion and politics, head straight to the compassion. Everything else is a distraction."

— Talib Kweli

"Our destiny is not written for us,
but by us."

— Barack Obama

"Our form of democracy is bribery, on the highest scale."

— Gore Vidal

"The first lesson of economics is scarcity: there is never enough of anything to fully satisfy all those who want it. The first lesson of politics is to disregard the first lesson of economics."

— Thomas Sowell

"You have summoned me in my weakness. You must sustain me in your strength."

— Franklin Pierce

"Fascism entirely agrees with Mr. Maynard Keynes, despite the latter's prominent position as a Liberal. In fact, Mr. Keynes' excellent little book, The End of Laissez-Faire (1926) might, so far as it goes, serve as a useful introduction to fascist economics. There is scarcely anything to object to in it and there is much to applaud."

— Benito Mussolini

"My fear was not of death itself, but a death without meaning."

— Huey Newton

"I read the newspapers avidly. It is my one form of continuous fiction."

— Aneurin Bevan

"I have come to realize that Jesse Helms stands for everything in politics that is anathema to me."

— William Weld

"Government cannot make man richer, but it can make him poorer."

— Ludwig von Mises

"I just received the following wire from my generous Daddy; Dear Jack, Don't buy a single vote more than is necessary. I'll be damned if I'm going to pay for a landslide."

— John F. Kennedy

"I'm sayin', why spend mine when I can spend yours?"

— Lil' Kim

"Every election is a sort of advance auction sale of stolen goods."

— H. L. Mencken

"The human being is in the most literal sense a political animal, not merely a gregarious animal, but an animal which can individuate itself only in the midst of society."

— Karl Marx

"Republicans understand the importance of bondage between a mother and child."

— Dan Quayle

"Next to fried foods, the South has suffered most from oratory."

— Brooks Hays

"I ain't rich, but Lord I'm free. Amarillo by morning, Amarillo is where I'll be."

— George Strait

"Finality is not the language of politics."

— Benjamin Disraeli

"The Koran is an inspiration for intolerance, murder and terror."

— Geert Wilders

"In times of crisis, it is of utmost importance to keep one's head."

— Unknown

"If only the left hated crime as much as they hated hate."

— William F. Buckley, Jr.

"We have no eternal allies, and we have not perpetual enemies. Our interests are eternal and perpetual, and those interests it is our duty to follow."

— Henry John Temple, 3rd Viscount Palmerston

"Presidents are selected, not elected."

— Franklin D. Roosevelt

"Power just makes you reject destiny and devour your fate."

— Big Pun

"I was elected by the women of Ireland, who instead of rocking the cradle, rocked the system."

— Mary Robinson

"No science is immune to the infection of politics and the corruption of power."

— Jacob Bronowski

"I don't know much about Americanism, but it's a damn good word with which to carry an election."

— Warren G. Harding

"The trouble with socialists is that they let their bleeding hearts go to their bloody heads."

— Tommy Douglas

"Modern society is hypnotized by socialism. It is prevented by socialism from seeing the mortal danger it is in. And one of the greatest dangers of all is that you have lost all sense of danger, you cannot even see where it's coming from as it moves swiftly towards you."

— Aleksandr Solzhenitsyn

"Politics is not about power. Politics is not about money. Politics is not about winning for the sake of winning. Politics is about the improvement of people's lives."

— Paul Wellstone

"Talk politics, talk about study and talk positively."

— Jiang Zemin

"I wear the black for the poor and the beaten down, Livin' in the hopeless, hungry side of town, I wear it for the prisoner who has long paid for his crime, But is there because he's a victim of the times. I wear the black for those who never read."

— Johnny Cash

"All might be free if they valued freedom, and defended it as they should."

— Samuel Adams

"There's another kind of poverty that only rich men know, a moral malnutrition that starves their very souls."

— Glenn Frey

"Greatest gift is human life and that we have a duty to protect the life of an unborn child."

— Ronald Reagan

"One of the great mistakes is to judge policies and programs by their intentions rather than their results."

— Milton Friedman

"Imagine, if you will, that I am an idiot. Then, imagine that I am also a Congressman. But, alas, I repeat myself."

— Mark Twain

"Few things are more irritating than when someone who is wrong is also very effective in making his point."

— Mark Twain

"Nothing that is morally wrong can be politically right."

— William E. Gladstone

"Our intent will not be to create gridlock. Oh, except maybe from time to time."

— Bob Dole

"Tolerance becomes a crime when applied to evil."

— Thomas Mann

"90% of the problem with marijuana is prohibition related, not use related."

— Gary Johnson

"A good politician is quite as unthinkable as an honest burglar."

— H. L. Mencken

"Rationalism belongs to the cool observer. But because of the stupidity of the average person, they follow not reason, but faith. This naïve faith, requires necessary illusions and emotionally potent oversimplifications, which are provided by the myth maker to keep the ordinary person on course."

— Reinhold Niebuhr

"The ones that you're calling wild are going to be the leaders in a little while."

— Johnny Cash

"You don't make the poor richer by making the rich poorer."

— Winston Churchill

"The single most important thing we want to achieve is for President Obama to be a one-term president."

— Mitch McConnell

"I can't talk politics with my cousin because he's such a hypocrite. He's against the death penalty and he hanged himself."

— Anthony Jeselnik

"Human rights are women's rights, and women's rights are human rights. Let us not forget that among those rights are the right to speak freely - and the right to be heard."

— Hillary Clinton

"When I am right, I get angry. Churchill gets angry when he is wrong. We are angry at each other much of the time."

— Charles de Gaulle

"We are the United States of Amnesia, we learn nothing because we remember nothing."

— Gore Vidal

"The bedfellows politics made are never strange. It only seems that way to those who have not watched the courtship."

— Marcel Achard

"We got a lot of politicians up there on Capital Hill. Ain't it funny how they prosper while the country stands still?"

— Waylon Jennings

"No society ever thrived because it had a large and growing class of parasites living off those who produce."

— Thomas Sowell

"The welfare state is not really about the welfare of the masses. It is about the egos of the elites."

— Thomas Sowell

"Forgiveness is abandoning your right to revenge."

— Desmond Tutu

"Politics is the entertainment branch of industry."

— Frank Zappa

"Overall relations between the North and the South have developed in favor of national reconciliation, unity and reunification."

— Kim Jong Il

"Murphy Brown is doing better than I am. At least she knows she still has a job next year."

— Dan Quayle

"It will not be any European statesman who will unite Europe: Europe will be united by the Chinese."

— Charles de Gaulle

"When politicians presume to do God's work, they do not become divine but diabolical."

— Pope Benedict XVI

"My deepest feeling about politicians is that they are dangerous lunatics to be avoided when possible and carefully humored; people, above all, to whom one must never tell the truth."

— W. H. Auden

"We live always under the weight of the old and odious customs. of our barbarous ancestors."

— Guy de Maupassant

"Meet them halfway with love, peace, and persuasion, and expect them to rise for the occasion."

— Van Morrison

"Are you better off today than you were four years ago?"

— Ronald Reagan

"I like a President who tells jokes
instead of appointing them."

— Bob Hope

"DELEGATION, n. In American politics, an article of merchandise that comes in sets."

— Ambrose Bierce

"If the book be false in its facts, disprove them; if false in its reasoning, refute it. But, for God's sake, let us freely hear both sides, if we choose."

— Thomas Jefferson

"We can't make any statements here. We can't talk about the internal politics of Paraguay."

— Alfredo Stroessner

"Avoid any specific discussion of public policy at public meetings."

— Quintus Tullius Cicero

"It is not enough to conquer; one must learn to seduce."

— Voltaire

"Russian Communism is the illegitimate child of Karl Marx and Catherine the Great."

— Clement Attlee

"Liberals feel unworthy of their possessions. Conservatives feel they deserve everything they've stolen."

— Mort Sahl

"Let us not despair but act. Let us not seek the Republican answer or the Democratic answer but the right answer. Let us not seek to fix the blame for the past - let us accept our own responsibility for the future."

— John F. Kennedy

"You were given the choice between war and dishonor. You chose dishonor and you will have war."

— Winston Churchill

"Don't confront me with my failures, I had not forgotten them."

— Jackson Browne

"You cannot spend your way out of recession or borrow your way out of debt."

— Daniel Hannan

"All within the state, nothing outside the state, nothing against the state."

— Benito Mussolini

"A heavy progressive or graduated income tax."

— Karl Marx

"It belongs to human nature to hate those you have injured."

— Tacitus

"It is easier to run a revolution than a government."

— Ferdinand Marcos

"Study the Constitution. Let it be preached from the pulpit, proclaimed in legislatures, and enforced in courts of justice."

— Abraham Lincoln

"If you are sure you understand everything that is going on, you are hopelessly confused."

— Walter F. Mondale

"There are no true friends in politics."

— Marcus Tullius Cicero

"The measure of the wealth of a nation is indicated by the measure of its protection of its industry; the measure of the poverty of a nation is marked by the degree in which it neglects and abandons the care of its own industry, leaving it exposed to the action of foreign powers."

— Henry Clay

"Ignore their heathen prayers and help us blow those little bastards straight to Hell. Amen."

— Hal Moore

"Walter Mondale has all the charisma of a speed bump."

— Will Durst

"Evil when we are in its power is not felt as evil but as a necessity, or even a duty."

— Simone Weil

"Never murder a man when he's busy committing suicide."

— Woodrow Wilson

"The unpleasant sound Bush is emitting as he traipses from one conservative gathering to another is a thin, tinny "arf" - the sound of a lap dog."

— George Will

"The problem isn't that Johnny can't read. The problem isn't even that Johnny can't think. The problem is that Johnny doesn't know what thinking is; he confuses it with feeling."

— Thomas Sowell

"The only just government is the government that serves its citizens, not itself."

— Timothy M. Dolan

"In politics, a lie unanswered
becomes truth within 24 hours."

— Willie Brown

"Maybe democrats will eventually turn on Obamacare when they realize you might need a photo I. D. to participate in the program."

— Dennis Miller

"I cannot undertake to lay my finger on that article of the Constitution which granted a right to Congress of expending, on objects of benevolence, the money of their constituents."

— James Madison

"You cannot help the poor by destroying the rich. You cannot lift the wage earner by pulling down the wage payer."

— Abraham Lincoln

"Members of Congress should be compelled to wear uniforms like NASCAR drivers, so we could identify their corporate sponsors."

— Caroline Baum

"As a general rule, I would say that human beings never behave more badly toward one another than when they believe they are protecting God."

— Barbara Brown Taylor

"The Liberals are the flying saucers of politics. No one can make head nor tail of them and they never are seen twice in the same place."

— John Diefenbaker

"Without equality there can be no democracy."

— Eleanor Roosevelt

"In politics, what begins in fear usually ends in folly."

— Samuel Taylor Coleridge

"A week is a long time in politics."

— Harold Wilson

"Politics is not predictions and politics is not observations. Politics is what we do. Politics is what we do, politics is what we create, by what we work for, by what we hope for and what we dare to imagine."

— Paul Wellstone

"The Righteous Mind: Why Good People are Divided by Politics and Religion."

— Jonathan Haidt

"Moral outrage is the most powerful motivating force in politics."

— Morton Blackwell

"A political convention is just not a place where you come away with any trace of faith in human nature."

— Murray Kempton

"Came out my mama's pussy, I'm on welfare. Twenty-six years old, still on welfare."

— Ol' Dirty Bastard

"Freedom is never more in peril than when politicians feel the pressure to 'do something. '."

— Sheldon Richman

"I wonder if it's possible to be a Republican and a Christian at the same time."

— Hillary Clinton

"Numerous politicians have seized absolute power and muzzled the press. Never in history has the press seized absolute power and muzzled the politicians."

— David Brinkley

"There are no favorites in my office. I treat them all with the same general inconsideration."

— Lyndon B. Johnson

"The best way to put more money
in people's wallets
is to leave it there in the first place."

— Edwin Feulner

"Wherever there is a jackboot stomping on a human face there will be a well-heeled Western liberal to explain that the face does, after all, enjoy free health care and 100 percent literacy."

— John Derbyshire

"You are pitiful isolated individuals;
you are bankrupts; your role is
played out. Go where you belong
from now on - into the dustbin of
history!"

— Leon Trotsky

"Self-regulation stands in relation to regulation the way self-importance stands in relation to importance."

— Willem Buiter

"The universal methodology of the tyrant is always incrementalism."

— Derek R. Audette

"How much easier it is to be critical than to be correct."

— Benjamin Disraeli

"There's no tragedy in life like the death of a child. Things never get back to the way they were."

— Dwight D. Eisenhower

"Government is too big and important to be left to the politicians."

— Chester Bowles

"I am not anti-American. But I am strongly pro-Canadian."

— John Diefenbaker

"Revolutions are always verbose."

— Leon Trotsky

"Politics is a pendulum whose swings between anarchy and tyranny are fueled by perennially rejuvenated illusions."

— Albert Einstein

"Those who believe religion and politics aren't connected don't understand either."

— Mahatma Gandhi

"If you want to succeed in politics you must keep your conscience firmly under control."

— David Lloyd George

"Politics is a jungle-torn between doing the right thing and staying in office."

— John F. Kennedy

"War gives the right to the conquerors to impose any condition they please upon the vanquished."

— Julius Caesar

"Today it is infinitely easier to kill one million people than to control one million people."

— Zbigniew Brzezinski

"I will not accept if nominated, and will not serve if elected."

— William Tecumseh Sherman

"Justice is the constant and eternal purpose that renders to each his due."

— Justinian I

"The art of statesmanship is to foresee the inevitable and to expedite its occurrence."

— Charles Maurice de Talleyrand

"The Left loves the poor so much it creates more of them every time it gets into power."

— Silvio Berlusconi

"Don't you get the idea I'm one of those goddam radicals. Don't get the idea I'm knocking the American system."

— Al Capone

"Global warming is too serious for the world any longer to ignore its danger or split into opposing factions on it."

— Tony Blair

"I love agitation and investigation and glory in defending unpopular truth against popular error."

— James A. Garfield

"Since the 1930s the technique of buying votes with the voters' own money has been expanded to an extent undreamed of by earlier politicians."

— Milton Friedman

"I know he'd be a poorer man if he never saw an eagle fly."

— John Denver

"Any nation that can survive what we have lately in the way of government, is on the high road to permanent glory."

— Molly Ivins

"I honestly believe I'd make one of the worst elected officials in the history of this country."

— Ross Perot

"Freedom of the press is guaranteed only to those who own one."

— A. J. Liebling

"Freedom is the by-product of economic surplus."

— Aneurin Bevan

"Profit sharing in the form of stock distributions to workers would help to democratize the ownership of America's vast corporate wealth which is today appallingly undemocratic and unhealthy."

— Walter Reuther

"Why, this fellow doesn't know any more about politics than a pig knows about Sunday."

— Harry S. Truman

"Always tell the truth. That way you don't have to remember what you said."

— Mark Twain

"They let dangerous men out of prison now, yes sir, I'm afraid it's so. Cause they're over crowded and it was only his fifth offense."

— Hank Williams, Jr.

"Being free is a state of mind."

— Lenny Kravitz

"A beast does not know that he is a beast, and the nearer a man gets to being a beast, the less he knows it."

— George MacDonald

"I don't like politics, hypocrites, folks with poodles."

— Alan Jackson

"Labour, like all other things which are purchased and sold. has its natural and its market price."

— David Ricardo

"The state remains, as it was in the beginning, the common enemy of all well-disposed, industrious and decent men."

— H. L. Mencken

"I have always felt that a politician is to be judged by the animosities he excites among his opponents."

— Winston Churchill

"Those who believe that politics and religion do not mix, understand neither."

— Albert Einstein

"The learned fool writes his nonsense in better language than the unlearned, but it is still nonsense."

— Benjamin Franklin

"Fascism is not in itself a new order of society. It is the future refusing to be born."

— Aneurin Bevan

"The way to stop discrimination on the basis of race is to stop discriminating on the basis of race."

— John Roberts

"If the authorities constrain banks and are aware of the activities of fringe banks and other financial institutions, they are in a better position to attenuate the disruptive expansionary tendencies of our economy."

— Hyman Minsky

"Every clique is a refuge for incompetence. It fosters corruption and disloyalty, it begets cowardice, and consequently is a burden upon and a drawback to the progress of the country. Its instincts and actions are those of the pack."

— Soong May-ling

"I have been underestimated for decades. I've done very well that way."

— Helmut Kohl

"If God wanted us to fly, He would have given us tickets."

— Mel Brooks

"Is it possible to be anything in this country without being a politician?"

— Martin Van Buren

"Everyone likes flattery; and when you come to Royalty you should lay it on with a trowel."

— Benjamin Disraeli

"Conservatism is the antidote to tyranny precisely because its principles are the founding principles."

— Mark Levin

"Voting is a civic sacrament."

— Theodore Hesburgh

"Being right too soon is socially unacceptable."

— Robert A. Heinlein

"Win or lose, we go shopping after the election."

— Imelda Marcos

"Revolutions are celebrated when they are no longer dangerous."

— Pierre Boulez

"No one can be, at the same time, a sincere Catholic and a true Socialist."

— Pope Pius XI

"Perfectionism, no less than isolationism or imperialism or power politics, may obstruct the paths to international peace. Let us not forget that the retreat to isolationism a quarter of a century ago was started not by a direct attack against international cooperation but against the alleged imperfections of the peace."

— Franklin D. Roosevelt

"Rhetoric is a poor substitute for action, and we have trusted only to rhetoric. If we are really to be a great nation, we must not merely talk; we must act big."

— Theodore Roosevelt

"A politician's words reveal less about what he thinks about his subject than what he thinks about his audience."

— George Will

"Why does Mosley always speak as though he were a feudal landlord abusing tenants who are in arrears with their rent ?"

— Clement Attlee

"Democracy can survive anything
except Democrats."

— Robert A. Heinlein

"If I speak, I am condemned. If I stay silent, I am damned!"

— Victor Hugo

"To err is human. To blame someone else is politics."

— Hubert H. Humphrey

"Steal a little and they throw you in jail Steal a lot and they make you king."

— Bob Dylan

"A politician is a person with whose politics you don't agree; if you agree with him he's a statesman."

— David Lloyd George

"No cause is left but the most ancient of all, the one, in fact, that from the beginning of our history has determined the very existence of politics, the cause of freedom versus tyranny."

— Hannah Arendt

"When extraordinary power and extraordinary pay are allotted to any individual in a government, he becomes the center, round which every kind of corruption generates and forms."

— Thomas Paine

"The Constitution was not written to restrain the citizen's behavior, it was writtne to restrain the government's behavior."

— Rand Paul

"One wanders to the left, another to the right. Both are equally in error, but, are seduced by different delusions."

— Horace

"It is an unfortunate human failing that a full pocketbook often groans more loudly than an empty stomach."

— Franklin D. Roosevelt

"The timid civilized world has found nothing with which to oppose the onslaught of a sudden revival of barefaced barbarity, other than concessions and smiles."

— Aleksandr Solzhenitsyn

"Live like the Kennedy's, above the law."

— Big Pun

"Constitution is for the people, people are not for the constitution. Change it for the betterment of the common man."

— Arvind Kejriwal

"Politics is very much like taxes - everybody is against them, or everybody is for them as long as they don't apply to him."

— Fiorello H. La Guardia

"It's a sin to be rich, but it's a low down shame to be poor."

— Lightnin' Hopkins

"Opinion has caused more trouble on this little earth than plagues or earthquakes."

— Voltaire

"The meaning of peace is the absence of opposition to socialism."

— Karl Marx

"The liquidation of colonialism is a trend of the times which no force can hold back."

— Kim Jong Il

"I never intend to adjust myself to the madness of militarism."

— Martin Luther King, Jr.

"Democracy cannot survive overpopulation."

— Isaac Asimov

"The moral consequences of totalitarian propaganda. are destructive of all morals because they undermind one of the foundations of all morals: the sense of and respect for truth."

— Friedrich August von Hayek

"We have never stopped sin by passing laws; and in the same way, we are not going to take a great moral ideal and achieve it merely by law."

— Dwight D. Eisenhower

"Liberals can't just come out and say, they want to take more of our money, kill babies, and discriminate on the basis of race."

— Ann Coulter

"Diplomats were invented simply to waste time."

— David Lloyd George

"And so it is in politics, dear brother, Each for himself alone, there is no other."

— Geoffrey Chaucer

"In republican governments, men are all equal; equal they are also in despotic governments: in the former, because they are everything; in the latter, because they are nothing."

— Baron de Montesquieu

"If those to whom power is delegated do well, they will be respected; if not, they will be despised."

— Thomas Paine

"Strugglin' and striving, that's how the dough come."

— Tupac Shakur

"A market economy is a tool - a valuable and effective tool - for organizing productive activity. A market society is a way of life in which market values seep into every aspect of human endeavour. It's a place where social relations are made over in the image of the market."

— Michael Sandel

"Have pity on a dinosaur."

— Hank Williams, Jr.

"Victory will never be found by taking the path of least resistance."

— Winston Churchill

"Socialism can only be put into practice only by methods which most socialists disapprove."

— Friedrich August von Hayek

"It doesn't say anywhere in the Constitution this idea of the separation of church and state."

— Sean Hannity

"After a time, civil servants tend to become no longer servants and no longer civil."

— Winston Churchill

"Socialism is inseparably interwoven with totalitarianism and the object worship of the state."

— Winston Churchill

"A Parliament is nothing less than a big meeting of more or less idle people."

— Walter Bagehot

"I'm often asked why I travel around the country talking politics. Is it for humanitarian reasons, community spirit, or is it for the money, the limousines or the girls? The answers are: no, no, yes yes yes!"

— Pat Paulsen

"Socialism is not an alternative to capitalism; it is an alternative to any system under which men can live as human beings."

— Ludwig von Mises

"What is conservatism? Is it not the adherence to the old and tried against the new and untried?"

— Abraham Lincoln

"We here highly resolve that these dead shall not have died in vain."

— Abraham Lincoln

"Minority conservatives hold a special place of gutter contempt in the minds of unhinged liberals, who can never accept the radical concept of a person of color rejecting identity politics."

— Michelle Malkin

"National defense is the sacred duty of the young and all other people."

— Kim Jong Il

"Good thing we've still got politics in Texas - finest form of free entertainment ever invented."

— Molly Ivins

"Republicans believe the best way to assure prosperity is to generate more jobs. The Democrats believe in more welfare."

— Ronald Reagan

"Parliament is not a congress of ambassadors from different and hostile interests; which interests each must maintain, as an agent and advocate, against other agents and advocates; but parliament is a deliberative assembly of one nation, with one interest, that of the whole; where, not local purposes, not local prejudices ought to guide, but the general good, resulting from the general reason of the whole. You choose a member indeed; but when you have chosen him, he is not a member of Bristol, but he is a member of parliament."

— Edmund Burke

"The most practical kind of politics
is the politics of decency."

— Theodore Roosevelt

"To get rich is glorious."

— Deng Xiaoping

"Treason doth never prosper.
What's the reason? Why, when it
prospers, none dare call it treason."

— John Harington

"The flag still stands for freedom
and they can't take that away."

— Lee Greenwood

"Politicians don't lie, they misspeak. And they don't steal, they mispocket."

— Robert Breault

"We defend and we build a way of life, not for America alone, but for all mankind."

— Franklin D. Roosevelt

"As long as I count the votes, what are you going to do about it?"

— Boss Tweed

"Politics and Religion are obsolete.
The time has come for Science and
Spirituality."

— Vinoba Bhave

"When they see me holding fish, they can see that I am comfortable with kings as well as with paupers."

— Imelda Marcos

"They say that women talk too much. If you have worked in Congress you know that the filibuster was invented by men."

— Clare Boothe Luce

"I was bold in the pursuit of knowledge, never fearing to follow truth and reason to whatever results they led, and bearding every authority which stood in their way."

— Thomas Jefferson

"Michael Moore simultaneously represents everything I detest in a human being and everything I feel obligated to defend in an American. Quite simply, it is that stupid moron's right to be that utterly, completely wrong."

— Dennis Miller

"I think it's a terrible shame that politics has become show business."

— Sydney Pollack

"I don't give a damn about the civilians."

— Richard M. Nixon

"I have never regarded politics as the arena of morals. It is the arena of interest."

— Aneurin Bevan

"Liberty is never safer than when politicans are terrified."

— Ted Cruz

"Politics is more difficult than physics."

— Albert Einstein

"There is no monopoly on common sense on either side of the political fence."

— Sting

"America has the best politicians money can buy."

— Will Rogers

"Hindu fundamentalism is a contradiction in terms, since Hinduism is a religion without fundamentals; there is no such thing as a Hindu heresy. How dare a bunch of goondas shrink the soaring majesty of the Vedas and the Upanishads to the petty bigotry of their brand of identity politics?"

— Shashi Tharoor

"Politics is the art of anesthesia."

— Mehmet Murat Ildan

"Osama, yo Mama didn't raise you right. When you were young, she must have wrapped your turban too tight."

— Ray Stevens

"Even when I was wrong, I got my point across."

— The Notorious B.I.G.

"To an intellectual who is adrift in politics, a theory is an aim; to a true politician his theory is a boundary."

— Francis Parker Yockey

"Simple logic tells you that if somebody wants you dead you have one course of action: To get them deader sooner."

— James Woods

"The only thing that saves us from bureaucracy is its inefficiency."

— Eugene McCarthy

"After all is said that can be said upon the liquor traffic, its influence is degrading upon the individual, the family, politics and business, and upon everything that you touch in this old world."

— Billy Sunday

"The President is always abused. If he isn't, he isn't doing anything."

— Harry S. Truman

"In this system, which tends to devour everything which stands in the way of increased profits, whatever is fragile, like the environment, is defenseless before the interests of a deified market, which become the only rule."

— Pope Francis

"There are few things more amusing in the world of politics than watching moderate Republicans charging to the right in pursuit of greater glory."

— Mario Cuomo

"What we anticipate seldom occurs; what we least expect generally happens."

— Benjamin Disraeli

"There are a lot of bad republicans; there are no good democrats."

— Ann Coulter

"It is not because a part of the government is elective, that makes it less a despotism, if the persons so elected, possess afterwards, as a parliament, unlimited powers. Election, in this case, becomes separated from representation, and the candidates are candidates for despotism."

— Thomas Paine

"Truth is the proper and sufficient antagonist to error, and has nothing to fear from the conflict, unless, by human interposition, disarmed of her natural weapons, free argument and debate; errors ceasing to be dangerous when it is permitted freely to contradict them."

— Thomas Jefferson

"Great ideology creates great times."

— Kim Jong Il

"Never judge a country by its politicians."

— Alfred Hitchcock

"Washington is the only place in the world where a gaffe is when a politician accidently speaks the truth."

— Charles Krauthammer

"The first lady is, and always has been, an unpaid public servant elected by one person, her husband."

— Lady Bird Johnson

"We don't want to go back to tomorrow, we want to move forward."

— Dan Quayle

"A Republican moves slowly. They are what we call conservatives. A conservative is a man who has plenty of money and doesn't see any reason why he shouldn't always have plenty of money. A Democrat is a fellow who never had any, but doesn't see any reason why he shouldn't have some."

— Will Rogers

"People say I'm indecisive, but I don't know about that."

— George H. W. Bush

"In inner-party politics, these methods lead, as we shall yet see, to this: the party organization substitutes itself for the party, the central committee substitutes itself for the organization, and, finally, a dictator substitutes himself for the central committee."

— Leon Trotsky

"Mistrust first impulses; they are
nearly always good."

— Charles Maurice de Talleyrand

"Amnesty is a terrible policy, and it's terrible politics. It's a terrible policy because you are rewarding people for breaking the law."

— Tom Tancredo

"A critical knowledge of the evolution of the idea of property would embody, in some respects, the most remarkable portion of the mental history of mankind."

— Lewis Henry Morgan

"I do not think the mere extension of the ballot a panacea for all the ills of our national life. What we need to-day is not simplymore voters, but better voters."

— Frances Harper

"Politics is applied biology."

— Ernst Haeckel

"Politics is a deleterious profession, like some poisonous handicrafts."

— Ralph Waldo Emerson

"Liberal institutions straightway cease being liberal the moment they are soundly established: Once this is attained, no more grievous and more thorough enemies of freedom exist than liberal institutions."

— Friedrich Nietzsche

"One blames politicians, not for inconsistency but for obstinacy. They are the interpreters, not the masters, of our fate. It is their job, in fact, to register the fact accompli."

— John Maynard Keynes

"By oft repeating an untruth, men come to believe it themselves."

— Thomas Jefferson

"A nation is a society united by a delusion about its ancestry and by common hatred of its neighbours."

— William Ralph Inge

"Since governments take the right of death over their people, it is not astonishing if the people should sometimes take the right of death over governments."

— Guy de Maupassant

"Remember one thing about democracy. We can have anything we want and at the same time, we always end up with exactly what we deserve."

— Edward Albee

"I would rather be a doorkeeper in the house of God than live in that palace at Washington."

— Rachel Jackson

"Let us not forget that we can never go farther than we can persuade at least half of the people to go."

— Hugh Gaitskell

"Cryptography shifts the balance of power from those with a monopoly on violence to those who comprehend mathematics and security design."

— Jacob Appelbaum

"No man could be equipped for the presidency if he has never been tempted by one of the seven cardinal sins."

— Eugene McCarthy

"The courts of kings are full of people, but empty of friends."

— Seneca the Elder

"The way to have power is to take it."

— Boss Tweed

"Senator John McCain could never convince me to vote for him. Only Hillary Clinton or Barack Obama can cause me to vote for McCain."

— Thomas Sowell

"I do the wrong, and first begin to brawl.
The secret mischiefs that I set abroach
I lay unto the grievous charge of others."

— William Shakespeare

"POW 369, I should salute you from this heart of mine. And thank you for placing your life on the line."

— Darryl Worley

"The struggle for the right to become politicians in itself made women into politicians."

— Eleanor Rathbone

"The time will come when human intelligence will rise to the mastery of property."

— Lewis Henry Morgan

"The history of American politics is littered with bodies of people who took so pure a position that they had no clout at all."

— Ben Bradlee

"Pledge allegiance to the flag that neglects us."

— Tupac Shakur

"Politics, as the word is commonly understood, are nothing but corruptions."

— Jonathan Swift

"Politics is the gizzard of society, full of gut and gravel."

— Henry David Thoreau

"We all know what Parliament is,
and we are all ashamed of it."

— Robert Louis Stevenson

"In Washington, DC, politics dominate even the most casual conversations."

— Armstrong Williams

"In politics nothing is so absurd as rancor."

— Camillo Benso, Count of Cavour

"Take our politicians: they're a bunch of yo-yos. The presidency is now a cross between a popularity contest and a high school debate, with an encyclopedia of cliches."

— Saul Bellow

"It is an axiom, enforced by all the experience of the ages, that they who rule industrially will rule politically."

— Aneurin Bevan

"Terrorism has become the systematic weapon of a war that knows no borders or seldom has a face."

— Jacques Chirac

"There is no act of treachery or meanness of which a political party is not capable; for in politics there is no honour."

— Benjamin Disraeli

"Our nation is well equipped to make the transition. We have an abundance of natural resources like wind, natural gas, solar and geothermal."

— Julia Gillard

"I'd rather have a German Division in front of me than a French one behind."

— George S. Patton

"Is there in all the history of human folly a greater fool than a clergymen in politics?"

— Pat Robertson

"Politics isn't only about government. Politics is about the people."

— Young Jeezy

"The revolution is carried out by means of one's thought, not through one's family background."

— Kim Jong Il

"We must recognize that we can't solve our problems now until there is a radical redistribution of economic and political power. a radical restructuring of the architecture of American society."

— Martin Luther King, Jr.

"If you don't like the President, it costs you 90 bucks to fly to Washington to picket. If you don't like the governor, it costs you 60 bucks to fly to Albany to picket. If you don't like me - 90 cents."

— Ed Koch

"The opposition is indispensable. A good statesman, like any other sensible human being, always learns more from his opposition than from his fervent supporters."

— Walter Lippmann

"The first rule of holes: When you're in one stop digging."

— Molly Ivins

"The good news is that, according to the Obama administration, the rich will pay for everything. The bad news is that, according to the Obama administration, you're rich."

— P. J. O'Rourke

"America is a nation with many flaws, but hopes so vast that only the cowardly would refuse to acknowledge them."

— James A. Michener

"I went to the UN and even the guidebook was spineless."

— Dennis Miller

"If Clinton had only attacked terrorism as much as he attacks George Bush we wouldn't be in this problem."

— Dennis Miller

"One ideological claim is that private property is theft, that the natural product of the existence of property is evil, and that private ownership therefore should not exist. What those who feel this way don't realize is that property is a notion that has to do with control - that property is a system for the disposal of power. The absence of property almost always means the concentration of power in the state."

— Daniel Patrick Moynihan

"Jesus was the first socialist, the first to seek a better life for mankind."

— Mikhail Gorbachev

"It's easier to criticize somebody else, than to see yourself."

— George Harrison

"Since Auschwitz we know what man is capable of. And since Hiroshima we know what is at stake."

— Viktor E. Frankl

"False greatness is unsociable and remote: conscious of its own frailty, it hides, or at least averts its face, and reveals itself only enough to create an illusion and not be recognized as the meanness that it really is. True greatness is free, kind, familiar and popular; it lets itself be touched and handled, it loses nothing by being seen at close quarters; the better one knows it, the more one admires it."

— Jean de la Bruyere

"He who would do good to another must do it in Minute Particulars: general Good is the plea of the scoundrel, hypocrite, and flatterer, for Art and Science cannot exist but in minutely organized Particulars."

— William Blake

"Secrecy, being an instrument of conspiracy, ought never to be the system of a regular government."

— Jeremy Bentham

"We hear war called murder. It is not; it is suicide."

— Ramsay MacDonald

"Conservatives define themselves in terms of what they oppose."

— George Will

"Socialism is a dead horse."

— Thorstein Veblen

"Born in iniquity and conceived in sin, the spirit of nationalism has never ceased to bend human institutions to the service of dissension and distress."

— Thorstein Veblen

"I still call myself a communist, because communism is no more what Russia made of it than Christianity is what the churches make of it."

— Pete Seeger

"My walk had purpose, my steps were quick and light, and I held firmly to what I felt was right."

— Bob Seger

"Being a conservative on campus is like bing a goat amongst the taliban. You are never safe."

— Greg Gutfeld

"Does politics have to be injected into everything?"

— Sargent Shriver

"Who defines terrorists? Today's terrorist is tomorrow's friend."

— Al Sharpton

"I want to preach a new doctrine. A complete separation of business and government."

— Franklin D. Roosevelt

"We are soldiers of the cross, we've been found to reach the lost."

— Randy Travis

"Those who vote decide nothing.
Those who count the vote decide
everything."

— Joseph Stalin

"All war must be just the killing of strangers against whom you feel no personal animosity; strangers whom, in other circumstances, you would help if you found them in trouble, and who would help you if you needed it."

— Mark Twain

"I don't believe your soul mate has to share your politics."

— Rachel Weisz

"The best government is a
benevolent tyranny tempered by an
occasional assassination."

— Voltaire

"All revolutions devour their own children."

— Ernst Rohm

"Politics is a game requiring great coolness."

— John A. Macdonald

"Affairs are easier of entrance than of exit; and it is but common prudence to see our way out before we venture in."

— Aesop

"The Aryan stock is bound to triumph."

— Winston Churchill

"The British Constitution has always been puzzling and always will be."

— Queen Elizabeth II

"In politics, nothing is contemptible."

— Benjamin Disraeli

"And if I am elected, I promise the formation of a new party, a third party, a wild party."

— Alice Cooper

"I've never been able to understand why a Republican contributor is a 'fat cat' and a Democratic contributor of the same amount of money is a 'public-spirited philanthropist'."

— Ronald Reagan

"The essence of statesmanship is not a rigid adherence to the past, but a prudent and probing concern for the future."

— Hubert H. Humphrey

"In chess the rules are fixed and the outcome is unpredictable, whereas in Putin's Russia the rules are unpredictable and the outcome is fixed."

— Garry Kasparov

"Every politician should have been born an orphan and remain a bachelor."

— Lady Bird Johnson

"The same prudence which in private life would forbid our paying our own money for unexplained projects, forbids it in the dispensation of the public moneys."

— Thomas Jefferson

"Blood is thicker than water, but politics are thicker than blood."

— Frank Herbert

"What do I bring to the Democratic National Convention that other reporters don't? Hair."

— Dave Mustaine

"You know, comrade Pachman, I don't enjoy being a Minister, I would rather play chess like you, or make a revolution in Venezuela."

— Che Guevara

"Dictators free themselves by enslaving others. They work not for your benefit, but their own."

— Charlie Chaplin

"The academic community has in it the biggest concentration of alarmists, cranks and extremists this side of the giggle house."

— William F. Buckley, Jr.

"I think the country has had enough Bushes."

— Barbara Bush

"Under every stone lurks a politician."

— Aristophanes

"Good can imagine Evil; but Evil cannot imagine Good."

— W. H. Auden

"It is fortunate that diplomats have long noses since they usually cannot see beyond them."

— Paul Claudel

"The cure for bad politics is the same as the cure for tuberculosis. It is living in the open."

— Woodrow Wilson

"The dictatorship of the Communist Party is maintained by recourse to every form of violence."

— Leon Trotsky

"Great nations are never impoverished by private, though they sometimes are by public prodigality and misconduct."

— Adam Smith

"Centralize property in the hands of a few and the millions are under bondage to property - a bondage as absolute and deplorable as if their limbs were covered with manacles. Abstract all property from the hands of labor and you thereby reduce labor to dependence; and that dependence becomes as complete a servitude as the master could fix upon his slave."

— Lewis Henry Morgan

"Pushers don't pay taxes."

— Big Daddy Kane

"I'd have all the cars made in the Carolinas, and I'd ban the ones made in China."

— Hank Williams, Jr.

"I'd put Hank Williams picture on one hundred dollar bills."

— Hank Williams, Jr.

"Nothing penetrates the liberal's sense of moral outrage."

— Bill Whittle

"If Communism was liberalism in a hurry, liberalism is Communism in slow motion."

— Joseph Sobran

"New opinions often appear first as jokes and fancies, then as blasphemies and treason, then as questions open to discussion, and finally as established truths."

— George Bernard Shaw

"If you have any interests you can gain a wider audience for those interests while the goldfish bowl is yours!"

— Eleanor Roosevelt

"In politics shared hatreds are almost always the basis of friendships."

— Alexis de Tocqueville

"The radical of one century is the conservative of the next. The radical invents the views. When he has worn them out, the conservative adopt."

— Mark Twain

"The whole basis of the United Nations is the right of all nations–great or small–to have weight, to have a vote, to be attended to, to be a part of the twentieth century."

— Adlai E. Stevenson

"Uncompromising thought is the luxury of the closeted recluse."

— Woodrow Wilson

"If U. S. foreign policy results in massive death and destruction abroad, we cannot feign innocence when some of that destruction is returned."

— Ward Churchill

"The purification of politics is an iridescent dream."

— John James Ingalls

"If Communism goes, I've still got the U. S. House of Representatives."

— Robert Novak

"There is nothing to which men cling more tenaciously than the privileges of class."

— Leonard Woolf

"Keynesians are to economics what witch doctors are to medicine."

— Peter Schiff

"Broadcasting is really too important to be left to the broadcasters."

— Tony Benn

"If there is one eternal truth of politics, it is that there are always a dozen good reasons for doing nothing."

— John le Carre

"It took a Clinton to clean up after the first Bush, it may take another Clinton to clean up after the second one."

— Hillary Clinton

"Whenever we defend democracy we find oil."

— Peter Gabriel

"The difference between a misfortune and a calamity is this: If Gladstone fell into the Thames, it would be a misfortune. But if someone dragged him out again, that would be a calamity."

— Benjamin Disraeli

"Socialism is the religion people get when they lose their religion."

— Richard John Neuhaus

"Liberalism is the transformation of mankind into cattle."

— Friedrich Nietzsche

"When you get too big a majority, you're immediately in trouble."

— Sam Rayburn

"A politician is not as narrow-minded as he forces himself to be."

— Will Rogers

"I have a very good family. I'm very fortunate to have a very good family. I believe very strongly in the family. It's one of the things we have in our platform, is to talk about it."

— Dan Quayle

"The man who can sing when he hasn't got a thing, he's the king of the whole wide world."

— Elvis Presley

"The Senate is a place filled with goodwill and good intentions, and if the road to hell is paved with them, then it's a pretty good detour."

— Hubert H. Humphrey

"Never answer a question from a farmer."

— Hubert H. Humphrey

"If we promise as public officials, we must deliver. If we as public officials propose, we must produce."

— Barbara Jordan

"Who watches the watchmen?"

— Juvenal

"In the contexts of religion and politics, words are not regarded as standing, rather inadequately, for things and events; on the contrary things and events are regarded as particular illustrations of words."

— Aldous Huxley

"There seem to me to be very few facts, at least ascertainable facts, in politics."

— Robert Peel

"There is something about a Republican that you can only stand him just so long; and on the other hand, there is something about a Democrat that you can't stand him quite that long."

— Will Rogers

"Both political parties have their good times and bad times, only they have them at different times."

— Will Rogers

"Politics is just like show business. You have a hell of an opening, coast for a while, and then have a hell of a close."

— Ronald Reagan

"Obama hasn't been working to earn reelection, he's been working to earn a spot on the PGA tour!"

— Mitch McConnell

"Never go out to meet trouble. If you just sit still, nine cases out of ten, someone will intercept it before it reaches you."

— Calvin Coolidge

"What we call 'morals' is simply blind obedience to words of command."

— Havelock Ellis

"A problem adequately stated is a problem well on its way to being solved."

— R. Buckminster Fuller

"Authority doesn't work without prestige, or prestige without distance."

— Charles de Gaulle

"More things in politics happen by accident or exhaustion than happen by conspiracy."

— Jeff Greenfield

"Patriotism corrupts history."

— Johann Wolfgang von Goethe

"Through talk, we tamed kings, restrained tyrants, averted revolution."

— Tony Benn

"Hope is the fuel of progress and fear is the prison in which you put yourself."

— Tony Benn

"Even Napoleon had his Watergate."

— Yogi Berra

"It is not socialist, as some of our critics contend. It isn't purely capitalist, either. It is a new way. A third way. A more humane, trusting, productive, exhilarating, and, in every sense, rewarding way."

— Ricardo Semler

"Of all manifestations of power, restraint impresses men most."

— Thucydides

"It is significant that the nationalization of thought has proceded everywhere pari passu with the nationalization of industry."

— Edward Hallett Carr

"Whoever has an army has power and that war decides everything."

— Mao Zedong

"I've seen many politicians paralyzed in the legs as myself, but I've seen more of them who were paralyzed in the head."

— George C. Wallace

"Socialism is a new form of slavery."

— Alexis de Tocqueville

"I never had a single conversation about politics with Ross Perot in my life; still haven't."

— James Stockdale

"He speaks to Me as if I was a public meeting."

— Queen Victoria

"A conservative is one who admires radicals centuries after they're dead."

— Leo Rosten

"Following rulers instead of prophets, the wicked can rule you, but the knowledge can stop it."

— Kool Moe Dee

"Laws cannot be imposed on him who is the master of the law."

— Benvenuto Cellini

"I believe that everything is political, and as such it should concern all of us. Authors who claim they don't deal with politics in their work are being naive, because even that is a political stance."

— Elena Poniatowska

"Currency warfare is the most destructive form of economic warfare."

— Harry Dexter White

"If allowed to continue, this process will turn the United States into a declining, unfair society with an impoverished, angry, uneducated population under the control of a small, ultrawealthy elite. Such a society would be not only immoral but also eventually unstable, dangerously ripe for religious and political extremism."

— Charles Ferguson

"It is much easier to modify an opinion if one has not already persuasively declared it."

— David Souter

"When the rich wage war, it's the poor who die."

— Jean-Paul Sartre

"There are occasions when the general belief of the people, even though it be groundless, works its effect as sure as truth itself."

— Friedrich Schiller

"My publicist told me not to talk about politics but, yes, I think we have a president who stole the election."

— Liev Schreiber

"The commonwealth of Athens is become a forest of beasts."

— William Shakespeare

"Crime, once exposed, has no refuge
but in audacity."

— Tacitus

"Im the lamest lame duck there could be."

— George C. Wallace

"The proof of liberal virtue is generousity with other people's money."

— George Will

"Virginia] has a very sizeable collection of democrats, liberals and moonbats. (Yes, they can be separated.)."

— John Ringo

"Revolutions never go backward."

— William H. Seward

"If politicians lived on praise and thanks they'd be forced into some other line of business."

— Edward Heath

"Politics is the art of the possible, the attainable — the art of the next best."

— Otto von Bismarck

"In the era of imperialism, businessmen became politicians and were acclaimed as statesmen, while statesmen were taken seriously only if they talked the language of succcessful businessmen."

— Hannah Arendt

"Politics is organized hatred, that is unity."

— John Jay Chapman

"Nancy, if I were your husband I'd drink it."

— Winston Churchill

"A)nything not acting as a propaganda arm for the Democrats or the Leftist agenda is considered conservative these days."

— Tammy Bruce

"No real social change has ever been brought about without a revolution. revolution is but thought carried into action."

— Emma Goldman

"Unlimited campaign spending eats at the heart of the democratic process."

— Barry Goldwater

"Geopolitics is all about leverage. We cannot make ourselves safer abroad unless we change our behavior at home."

— Thomas Friedman

"Reading musses up my mind."

— Henry Ford

"Liberals dispute that Reagan won the Cold War on the basis of their capacity to put mocking quotation marks around the word, won. That's pretty much the full argument: Restate a factual proposition with sneering quote marks."

— Ann Coulter

"Do what thou wilt shall be the whole of the law."

— Aleister Crowley

"A sophistical rhetorician, inebriated with the exuberance of his own verbosity, and gifted with an egotistical imagination that can at all times command an interminable and inconsistent series of arguments to malign an opponent and to glorify himself."

— Benjamin Disraeli

"There they are. See no evil, hear no evil, and. evil."

— Bob Dole

"Governments tend not to solve problems, only to rearrange them."

— Ronald Reagan

"The kind of violence, looting, destruction that we saw from a handful of individuals in Baltimore, there's no excuse for that. That's not a statement. That's not politics. That's not activism. That's just criminal behavior."

— Barack Obama

"The results of political changes are hardly ever those which their friends hope or their foes fear."

— Thomas Huxley

"Of all sciences there is none where first appearances are more deceitful than in politics."

— David Hume

"Government as well as religion has furnished its schisms, its persecutions and its devices for fattening idleness on the earnings of the people."

— Thomas Jefferson

"One single object . [will merit] the endless gratitude of the society: that of restraining the judges from usurping legislation."

— Thomas Jefferson

"Political institutions are a superstructure resting on an economic foundation."

— Vladimir Lenin

"When religion and politics ride in the same cart, the whirlwind follows."

— Frank Herbert

"This was a good example of the fascist policing of public discourse in this country by nominal liberals who have become as unthinkingly wedded to dogma as any junior member of the Spanish Inquisition."

— Camille Paglia

"I'm not a member of an organized party. I'm a Democrat."

— Will Rogers

"If experience teaches us anything at all, it teaches us this: that a good politician, under democracy, is quite as unthinkable as an honest burglar."

— H. L. Mencken

"Above all, there is no exception to this rule: that the idea of political superiority always resolves itself into the idea of psychological superiority."

— Friedrich Nietzsche

"Party leads to vicious, corrupt and unprofitable legislation, for the sole purpose of defeating party."

— James F. Cooper

"If a tax cut increases government revenues, you haven't cut taxes enough."

— Milton Friedman

"To rule is easy, to govern difficult."

— Johann Wolfgang von Goethe

"Ownership by delegation is a contradiction in terms. When men say, for instance (by a false metaphor), that each member of the public should feel himself an owner of public property-such as a Town Park-and should therefore respect it as his own, they are saying something which all our experience proves to be completely false. No man feels of public property that it is his own; no man will treat it with the care of the affection of a thing which is his own."

— Hilaire Belloc

"The Reformation has been called in a biting epigram "a rising of the rich against the poor. "."

— Hilaire Belloc

"It is a general rule of human nature that people despise those who treat them well, and look up to those who make no concessions."

— Thucydides

"So the starting point and the basis of their liberal wails of anguish always and always is guilt. Guilt, guilt, guilt."

— John Ringo

"There will never be a really free and enlightened state until the state comes to recognize the individual as a higher and independent power, from which all its own power and authority are derived."

— Henry David Thoreau

"Everyone is always in favour of general economy and particular expenditure."

— Anthony Eden

"Giving votes in exchange for ideological support. To wit: identity politics for homosexuals."

— Harry Hay

Made in the USA
Columbia, SC
07 August 2024

5e5af663-9313-4d29-b04a-00c84f29dbd8R01